STUDIO VISTA

Light in Watercolour

PATRICIA MONAHAN

STUDIO
VISTA

ACKNOWLEDGEMENTS
The author and publishers would like to thank the following artists who have
allowed us to use their work in this book: Charles Bartlett, p. 80; Francis Bowyer,
p. 22; Trevor Chamberlain, pp. 52–3, 88–9; David Curtis, p. 93; Shirley Felts,
pp. 19, 25, 69; Sarah Holliday, pp. 5, 32, 33; Sophie Knight, p. 51; John Lidzey,
pp. 8, 9, 81; Ian Sidaway, pp. 75, 92; Adrian Smith, p. 91; Stan Smith, pp 14, 15,
17, 23, 24, 35, 40, 41, 43; Tig Sutton, pp. 94–5; Grahame Sydney, p. 74;
Bill Taylor, pp. 88, 93.

Special thanks are also due to Winsor & Newton for technical advice and their
generous help with materials; and to Adrian Smith, pp. 62, 64, 90; Stan Smith,
pp. 10, 16, 36, 40, 48, 54, 70; Albany Wiseman, pp. 76, 82, 85; and Francis Bowyer,
pp. 26, 58; for step-by-step demonstrations.

Studio Vista
a Cassell imprint
Wellington House
125 Strand
London WC2R 0BB

Series editors Jenny Rodwell and Patricia Monahan
The moral rights of the author have been asserted

Series designer Edward Pitcher

Distributed in the United States by
Sterling Publishing Co. Inc.
387 Park Avenue South, New York, NY 10016–8810

Distributed in Australia by
Capricorn Link (Australia) Pty Ltd
2/13 Carrington Road, Castle Hill, NSW 2154

British Library Cataloguing in Publication Data
A catalogue record for this book is available from the British Library

ISBN 0-289-80123-0

Typeset by Litho Link Ltd, Welshpool, Powys, Wales
Printed and bound in Great Britain
by Bath Colour Books Ltd

CONTENTS

Light . . . and dark

●

▶ 'Plum Blossom' by Sarah Holliday. By playing with the way light reveals and conceals forms, the artist has created an image that is coolly beautiful and rigorously composed. The twigs and shadows form a zigzag that holds the composition together. 'I was intrigued by the overall geometry of the composition, which had a non-geometric form as its main focus,' she says. A narrow slit of light was falling through the blossom, illuminating parts of it while putting others in shadow.

WHEN ASKED BY Boswell, 'Sir, what is poetry?', Dr Johnson replied, 'Why Sir, it is much easier to say what it is not. We all *know* what light is; but it is not easy to *tell* what it is.'

You can't touch it, you can't taste it, you can't hear it, but it is this nebulous, insubstantial and difficult-to-understand 'thing' that allows us to see. It gives us a visual world, allowing us to discern colour and form, and even mood. All visual art depends on the ability to see, and much of it is concerned with expressing aspects of light in some form – a challenge that absorbs, puzzles, exasperates and sometimes confounds the artist.

This book is an attempt to capture this most elusive of phenomena, to find out what it is, what it does and how you can exploit and render it in watercolour. I have concentrated on particular aspects of light and have asked artists to explain in their own words what light means to them.

▼ This pencil drawing is Sarah Holliday's first response to the subject and is the basis for the work opposite.

●

4

TECHNIQUES

SEEING TONE

Ask anyone to complete the phrase 'light and . . .' and they will invariably supply the word 'dark'. It is really this contradictory relationship that we have in mind when we think of light. Where light isn't, there is dark. The transition between light and dark gives us tone, the gradations of lightness and darkness, which is one of the ways we see and understand forms, and describe them in our paintings and drawings.

Tone is a difficult concept to grasp at first, but if you look at a black-and-white photograph in a newspaper, you will see that you get almost as much information from it as you would from a colour photograph of the same subject. This is because the areas of black, white and grey (dark tones, highlights and half-tones) allow you to understand the depth and space within the picture and the bulk and solidity of objects.

Look around you now, and try and see your surroundings in terms of light and dark areas. Initially, it is very difficult to see tone because colours, patterns, shadows, reflected light and different light sources interfere and cause confusion. If you screw up your eyes, it will be easier. Now make a quick sketch, blocking in patches of light and dark tone, with three shades of grey. It will help if you can forget what you are looking at and try to see the subject purely as an abstract. Remember that the white of the paper gives you your lightest tone, so save that for highlights or very light colours. Work quickly and don't worry about what the result will look like. When you've finished, you'll be surprised to find that a convincing image emerges from the patches of tone.

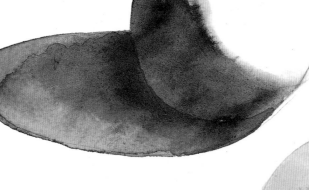

▼ The tone of colour
In these four spheres tone is used to describe form and colour. The side away from the light is darkest, but if you compare this with the single orange on the left you will see that the lightest area is a pale grey rather than the white of the paper. The grey implies a colour.

▲ Light, tone and shadow
An orange is placed in a strong directional light. It blocks the beam of light so that the light does not illuminate the side away from the light source; this is in shadow. The orange also throws a cast shadow on the horizontal surface of the table. This is darkest at the centre and fades towards the edge. Notice the way the cast shadow helps to establish the ground on which the object is standing.

Surprisingly, you can even get an idea of the colour of objects, because colour has a tonal value. Find a group of coloured objects – children's building bricks or a pile of books perhaps – and put them together on the floor. Now study them through half-closed eyes. You will find that yellow objects are lighter in tone than red ones, but that some shades of different colours are very similar in tone. In some cases it is extremely difficult to decide which colour is lighter and which is darker, and if you set your family the same task they will agree about some relationships and hotly dispute others.

▶ **Light, tone, shadow, colour and texture**
In this image we have a more ambitious use of tone. There are lights, darks and shadows, but there are also cross-shadows cast by light coming from different directions. The dark areas aren't consistently dark because light is reflected back from other surfaces. Notice that the lightest area is the white of the paper.

▼ **Using four tones**
Here four tones have been used to describe the form and local colour of the balls. Try this exercise. Mix up four shades of grey and use these tones to paint a simple subject like a ball or a cup.

7

▼ *Here we have two studies of the same subject by the artist John Lidzey. On this page an interior is dealt with in terms of light and dark. The artist has used black Conté crayon. The white of the paper stands for the lightest areas, where the light coming through the window falls on the seat of the chair and the top of the table, and the top of the chest of drawers. The darkest tones are created by overlaying layers of hatched Conté. For the mid-tones between the darkest and lightest areas, he has used a web of loosely worked hatching.*

▶ *On the facing page the same subject is now interpreted in watercolour. The artist has captured the sense of an enclosed interior space that is illuminated by warm light filtering through the window. Areas like the wall behind the chest of drawers are warmed by the sunlight, while the areas in shadow have a cool, blue tinge.*

The artist handles watercolour with evident confidence and enjoyment, allowing the paint and the support to do part of the work. In some places washes flow and melt to create ambiguous veils of colour; in others 'accidental' puddles and streaks contribute to a paint surface which acknowledges the special qualities and beauty of watercolour.

ROOFSCAPE

One of the traditional concerns of most Western art is the depiction of a three-dimensional world on a two-dimensional surface. Artists are illusionists and use a repertoire of tricks to convince spectators that the rectangle of the picture contains space, relief surfaces and solid forms. Artists need to see and understand light and tone in the real world in order to exploit it convincingly in the 'unreal' illusionist world of their pictures.

Our first project is a subject that will be readily available – a view out of a window. In this case, the jumble of rooftops might seem daunting, but simply draw what you see, using your pencil to assess the relationship between one distance and another. The glazing bars of the window will provide you with a useful drawing grid.

This is not a romantic or sentimental image, but what you have is an abstract arrangement of angles, horizontal and vertical lines and geometric shapes. The contrast of light and dark tones and intense shadows adds another set of graphic forms onto the existing architectural shapes.

The colour range too is limited: closely related brown-reds for the tiles and purplish-blue for the slates, interspersed with patches of complementary greens giving the subject a sense of unity.

Stan Smith started by breaking the picture down into areas of light, tone and shadow, creating an abstract arrangement of shapes and patterns.

He used a limited palette of five colours: Hooker's green, chrome yellow, ultramarine blue, light red and Payne's grey.

You can copy this step-by-step study of rooftops, but it would be much better to find a similar subject. By looking out of the windows or doors of your home, you will find in most cases an equivalent subject; if it's not a roofscape, you may have a view of outbuildings, or the backs of buildings opposite, or even fire escapes, all providing interesting architectural themes that can be studied under different light conditions.

▲ **1** *The subject is superficially daunting – a higgeldy-piggeldy pattern of steeply pitched roofs, dormer windows and tall chimneys topped with a forest of chimney pots. Study the subject and see it as a collection of various abstract geometric shapes. These underlying geometric shapes, together with the overlaid geometry of the patterns of light and dark, and the subtleties of the warm earth reds all provide the hook for the picture.*

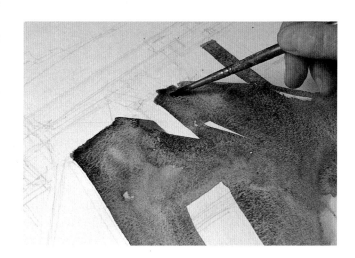

▲ **2** *The artist started with a drawing made with an HB pencil. Spend some time on your drawing, using a pencil to assess the relationships between shapes. By holding your pencil up at arm's length you can measure the angles of the eaves and the slope of the roofs. Look carefully, see how horizontals and verticals relate to each other, measure and judge relationships by eye.*

To simplify this project the artist started by washing in the darkest tones, using a mixture of Payne's grey cooled with ultramarine for a bluish neutral colour. Wash in the colour but don't labour it. Make it a little darker than you intend because watercolour dries lighter.

▶ **3** *The trick is to try not to make the drawing too architectural. Look at the work of people who use architectural details in their work and you'll find that they don't make it look mechanical.*

The drawing must be considered and reconsidered all the way through. Don't simply trace with the paint. Keep on looking to see if the image needs adjustment; here, the artist found that some of the proportions weren't quite right. Realizing that you are not simply 'colouring in' keeps you on your toes. Questioning the decisions you made earlier will ensure that the drawing is a living, evolving thing.

▶ **4** *Now the artist starts to wash in colour, working boldly and broadly with a No. 10 brush. He uses a range of reds mixed from Venetian red and burnt sienna to create variations on the local colour. By using a big brush he stops himself from getting too tight. Try to keep to a general feel of the tones and the colours.*

▲ **5** *Don't focus on one part of the painting, try and keep the whole thing going, constantly assessing the tonal arrangements in the subject to see that you get those right in the picture. Screw up your eyes to simplify the subject and exaggerate the tonal contrasts.*

Here, the artist introduced some of the foliage in the background.

▲ **6** *Here you can see how loosely and broadly the colour has been applied. Notice how the crisp contrasts of tone along the ridges of the roofs and on the sides of the chimney, all contribute towards the sense of bright light. The darks make the lights seem brighter.*

11

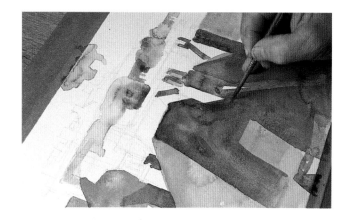

◄ **7** *Using a smaller brush – No. 6 – the artist adds emphasis here and there, adjusting the tones, playing up the contrasts and amending the drawing.*

▼ **8** *Here he develops the background, simplifying and enjoying the way the paint pools and puddles, letting the paint create its own equivalents of reality.*

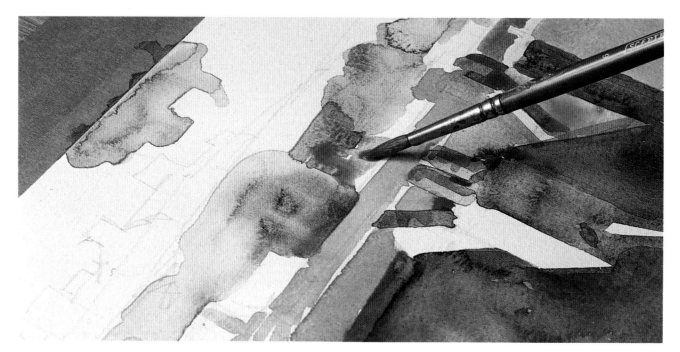

◄ **9** *It is important to stand back and contemplate your work at regular intervals, judging it against the subject and assessing it as an image in its own right. Make any adjustments that will make it a better picture, leaving things out or moving them about if they improve the composition.*

◀ **10** *Some rich red – Venetian red – is washed over a roof, creating an area of bright colour.*

▼ **11** *Avoid the temptation to make the image too architectural; focus instead on pattern and colour. The artist has added some crisp details with the tip of the No. 6 brush. You don't need a lot of brushes. Because a good brush comes to a point, you can get a lot of detail even with quite a large brush. Notice the way the artist has indicated the edge of the ridge tiles and the details on the dormers and within the windows by adding just enough to suggest the forms, but avoiding the temptation to pull them into too sharp a focus.*

LIGHT AND SHADOW

Shadow should not be confused with tone. Shadow is an area of darkness that is created by an object standing between the light and the surface beneath or adjacent to it. By screwing up your eyes you will see that shadows also have tonal value. Shadows cast on to the subject give you clues about form. For example, if a figure is placed in front of a window in full sunlight, the dark bands of the shadows of the glazing bars will be cast over the figure and will be displaced around the undulations of the form, emphasizing and helping to describe those forms.

Shadow also gives you useful information about the direction and quality of light in a setting. On a bright sunlit day there will be a strong contrast between the areas in full light and those in shadow; on an overcast day there will be less contrast, or possibly no perceptible shadow at all.

So how do you render shadows? The obvious

▲ *'Carnival' by Stan Smith. In this study of costumed revellers at Venice's annual carnival, the artist has used backlighting and cast shadows to heighten the drama of the scene. He juxtaposes light and dark, dark and light, so that in some places the forms are negative shapes and in others they are positives. The image was worked up from photographs and sketchbook notes jotted down on the spot. He has used gouache and watercolour, overlaid with crayon, to create a complex web of colour.*

solution might seem to be just to put in a bit of black or a dark colour. In the late nineteenth century, however, it was discovered that the relationship between light and colour is exceedingly complex. Shadows were found to contain a great deal of colour – often the complementary, or opposite, colour of the object casting the shadow (see pages 24–25).

This influenced the work of the Impressionists, and you will find that shadows in their paintings are complex areas of broken and layered colour, containing colour reflected from the surrounding area, plus the complementary. So rather than being areas of flat colour, these shadows have a scintillating luminosity that enlivens the painting and effectively mirrors the complexity of natural light.

Make careful assessments of the degree of contrast between areas in shadow and adjacent areas, whether shaded or illuminated, and study the quality of the edges. These things tell you a lot about the quality of the light, the time of day and the distance of the object casting the shadow from the shadow. Bright light casts crisp shadows, while the shadows cast by diffuse light have softer, less defined edges. Only when the sun is directly overhead do shadows appear directly under horizontal surfaces such as the canopies of trees, the seats of chairs or awnings, and vertical objects such as telegraph poles or standing figures cast almost no shadow at all. But during the short evenings late in the year, when the sun hangs low on the horizon, you get immensely long shadows. And on a clear winter's day, when the sun is glittering and bright, the effect of the long, crisp shadows cast by trees, cattle and figures adds drama to the landscape.

◄ *'Evening Light' by Stan Smith. This image was painted when the sun was low in the sky and threw this tree into dramatic silhouette casting a strong dark shadow. This viewpoint shows the tree and its shadow as a single monolithic form.*

The artist made the image on a blue tinted paper, which captured the coolness of the evening light and provides a foil for the warm summer greens. He interpreted the subject freely, laying colour on then washing and blotting it off to create interesting shapes and textures.

TECHNIQUES

PAINTING SHADOWS

There are two important 'don'ts' when dealing with shadows. First, don't add shadows as an after-thought. You can't grasp them or feel their shape, so it is sometimes tempting to leave them out or add them at the end of the painting. But they are important features of our visual world, even though they don't occupy three-dimensional space or feature in the tactile world. So treat shadows as part of the composition.

Second, don't paint shadows black. If you do, they will look solid and opaque, whereas in reality they should have depth and form just like other areas of the painting. Our environment is full of reflected light that bounces off adjacent objects, modifying local colour, tone and shadows. Nothing is ever what you think it is or what it seems at first glance. Look for the colour in shadow areas and paint what you see. You will find that you create

▶ **1** *This is the original study, made on the spot, of people taking the summer sun. I asked the artist to re-create the chairs and shadows, to see how he achieved the richness and transparency of that area.*

◀ **2** *First the ground is laid in freely with yellows and greens to get a richness throughout. The artist used cadmium medium, lemon yellow and also strong viridian green, overlaying the colours to create an effective grassy ground with a little dappling in it.*

To get transparency into the shadows, he lays them in with Winsor green, a bluish, transparent green. Then he uses a pencil to draw the forms of the deckchairs.

shadows that have luminosity and depth and your paint surface will be varied and interesting.

Here we look at the way Stan Smith has tackled the shadows in a sketch of a riverside scene with the sun shining on figures sitting in deckchairs. It is a pleasing and intriguing theme. The light shines through the fabric, silhouetting the seated forms, and causes the seats to cast shadows. The shadows are treated as important elements in the composition. They are seen as definite shapes and are drawn with the same conviction as the 'real' objects such as chairs and figures.

The brilliance of a hot summer's day is expressed by the brightness of the water, the dark and emphatic shapes of the shadows and the richness of the colour throughout – especially in the shadows.

▶ **3** *The stripes of the deckchairs are laid in with a soft coloured pencil.*

▼ **4** *The freshness of the paint and the crispness of the patches of colour, plus the tonal contrasts, capture the qualities of green grass lit by sunlight.*

Colour and composition

COLOUR IS AN exciting and magical phenomenon. Mysterious, perplexing and constantly changing, it provides artists with their greatest thrills . . . and greatest challenges.

Everything we can see has a colour, even if it is black and white, or grey. You can't paint colour until you learn really to 'see' it. When you start looking at the world with the eyes of an artist, you'll find that things aren't what you thought they were! Black isn't simply black: there are warm reddish blacks, transparent blacks and cool blue-blacks. The yellow of a lemon is different from the yellow of a banana or a melon. Flesh isn't pink, grass isn't always green and the sky is only rarely blue!

Good pictures don't just happen; they are made or composed. Artists organize the elements of light, tone and colour within the rectangle of the support in order to create an image that has unity and impact, and effectively expresses whatever they are trying to communicate. Composition is about making decisions, selecting, editing and emphasizing in order to create an image that you find satisfying.

'Tulips' by Shirley Felts. The artist has used carefully controlled washes of fresh, clear watercolour to build up this exuberant picture of tulips. The delicate, bright colours of the flowers make considerable demands on the artist, who must keep the colours fresh, yet orchestrate all the tonal values so that the characteristic forms of the flower heads are depicted accurately.

In this painting Shirley has drawn attention to the decorative qualities of the subject, cropping in close to emphasize the patterns made by the flowers on the picture plane. The background is densely patterned, forcing itself on to the picture plane so that the spatial elements are played down.

TECHNIQUES

THE LANGUAGE OF COLOUR

Your ability to use colour will improve immensely if you understand some of the basic concepts of colour theory. The colour wheel or colour circle is a device that makes understanding colour and colour relationships easy. It also helps you to remember some of the terms.

The first three colours to look at are the *primaries*: red, yellow and blue. These are important because they cannot be mixed on the palette from other colours and, in theory, every other colour can be mixed from them.

Separating them, you will find orange, green and violet. These are called the *secondaries*, because they are derived from the primaries: red and yellow give orange; yellow and blue give green; red and blue give violet.

The *tertiaries* are produced by adding a primary to a secondary. They are useful colours like bluish green and yellowy green; reddish orange and reddish violet.

Every colour has four qualities: hue, tone, intensity and temperature. Artists use the word *hue* rather than colour to describe a pure colour, a colour that has not been lightened or darkened in any way. *Tone* describes the lightness or darkness of a colour. A *shade* is a hue that has been darkened; a *tint* is a hue that has been lightened. *Intensity* describes the purity, brilliance or saturation of a colour. The most intense green is the purest, brightest green possible. As soon as you start mixing hues, you reduce their intensity.

All colours have a *temperature*. Some colours look warm and others look cool, and there is a general consensus about which is which. Here the colour wheel is helpful. It can be divided into two halves. In one half we find the warm colours: yellows, reds and oranges. On the other side are the cool colours: blues, violets and greens.

cool colours

mixture

French ultramarine

cerulean blue

mixture

alizarin crimson

cadmium red

warm colours

mixture

cadmium yellow pale

lemon yellow

TECHNIQUES

EXPLOITING COLOUR TEMPERATURE

Colour temperature refers to the degree of warmth or coldness of a colour. This concept is invaluable to the artist. However, colour temperature is relative, so you'll find that some yellows are warmer than others. If you look at the colour wheel, you'll find that the pairs of pigments I have selected can be classed as warm or cool. Taking the reds, alizarin crimson is cooler than cadmium red, which has an orange bias, whereas the blue of ultramarine is cooler than cerulean blue, which has a greenish bias.

The temperature of colours has several practical applications for artists. First, there is the psychological aspect of colour: colour can be used to create mood in a painting. The warm colours are associated with energy, heat and aggression, with sunlight and fire. Cool colours are more tranquil and relaxing; they are typically the colours of snow, sea and sky, and moonlight. These associations are very strong. In one experiment people in a blue room set their central heating thermostat four degrees higher than others in a red room even though the temperature in both rooms was the same. Exposure to red has been shown to increase muscular tension, respiration, heart rate, blood pressure and brain activity. Blue has the opposite effect, and can make you feel relaxed and quite sleepy. If you want your painting to express heat and excitement, you would naturally tend to select reds, oranges and warm earth colours. A chilly winter landscape or a sad, introspective image would call for a cooler palette.

Colour also affects our spatial perceptions. Warm colours are said to advance, while cool colours recede. Place a patch of red and a similar-sized patch of blue on a canvas. The red will draw the eye and appear to be located further forward on the picture plane. It will also appear to take up more space than the patch of blue.

Interior designers use colour to make rooms seem larger or smaller, to make a ceiling seem higher or lower. By painting the walls of a large room in a rich red or russet, you can make them close in so that the room feels small and cosy. Conversely, pale blue can be used to visually push back the walls of a small room so that it feels more spacious and airy.

These qualities can be manipulated to enhance the illusion of three-dimensional space. Cool colours are used on the horizon, and warmer colours in the foreground in order to suggest the effect of recession and depth in a picture.

You can also use colour as a compositional device, drawing attention to an important feature by adding a touch of a colour that is warmer than the surrounding colour. As temperature is relative, a touch of ultramarine will sing out in a field of cool cerulean or Prussian blue. Warm colours are also insistent. A small touch of scarlet will be sufficient to enliven quite a large area of green.

▲ *In this painting by Francis Bowyer, the figure is seen* 'contre-jour', *against the light. The light throws the figure of the child, the table and chair into dramatic silhouette. The contrast between the cool blue shadows and the warm yellows and ochres in the areas of direct sunlight heightens the sense of brightness and warmth. Notice that the shadows have a definite colour value; they are not painted black or grey.*

▲ In this painting of the Rialto Bridge in Venice, Stan Smith has used cool blues and greys to create an image that captures the watery, otherworldly atmosphere of the city. The colours used are primarily cool, but the energy of the paint application, combined with the touches of yellow and vivid red gives the painting a liveliness.

23

TECHNIQUES

EXPLOITING OPPOSITES

Probably the most important colour 'relationship' is between complementary pairs – the colours that appear opposite each other on the colour wheel. It was only in the nineteenth century that scientists really began to understand how complementary colours affected each other, although artists have always been intuitively aware of the power of the relationship. This can be seen in the work of the Old Masters, particularly in the juxtaposition of complementary pinks and greens to create lively flesh tones.

The complementary of a primary is always a secondary, and the complementary of a secondary is the primary not included in its mixture. The six-colour colour wheel gives you the following complementary pairs: red–green; blue–orange; yellow–violet.

One of the most dramatic manifestations of the power of the complementary relationship is the 'afterimage'. Try this experiment. Paint a square of red on a sheet of paper. Stare at the red square fixedly for at least ten seconds from a distance of about 50 centimetres. Now quickly transfer your gaze to the sheet of white paper. Almost immediately a greenish afterimage of the square will appear. If you repeat the exercise with the green square, you will see a pinkish afterimage, while the afterimage of the yellow square is pale violet.

Complementary colours are important to artists because they do two important and apparently contradictory things. When placed side by side they enhance each other; and when mixed together they neutralize each other.

In the first case, because complementary colours offer each other the maximum contrast, colours appear most intense when placed alongside their complementary partner. Green looks its greenest when contrasted with a complementary red; blue looks bluer when it is contrasted with orange. This has many practical applications. By introducing a touch of the complementary into an area, you can make that area richer and more vibrant – touches of earth red will make grass or foliage look brighter.

In the second case, complementary pairs can be mixed together to create a range of beautiful greys (cool neutrals) and browns (warm neutrals), very different from the rather dull shades produced by mixing black and white. Experiment with mixes of red and green, blue and orange, yellow and violet. By adjusting the proportions of each, you will produce a wonderful range of warm and cool neutrals, earthy pinks and browns and pearly lilacs and greys. Use these colours in shadows, flesh tones and as a foil for more strident colours. Study the work of the great colourists like Walter Sickert (1860–1942), and you will find that these coloured or neutral greys play an important part. If a colour seems strident, you can 'knock it back' by adding a touch of its complementary.

◄ *In this painting of a woman with a washing bowl, brilliant sunlight floods in through an open window, creating striking patterns of light and dark on the figure. The figure is the focus of the painting, but the artist, Stan Smith, draws attention to the still life on the table by carefully balancing the red of the bowl with the complementary green of the bottle.*

▲ *'The Wicker Chair in Autumn' by Shirley Felts. In this delightful painting the artist captures the particular light of a sunny autumn day. The glorious golds and oranges of the foliage are set off perfectly by cool shadows in complementary blues and lilacs, giving the painting a shimmering quality and providing a pleasing balance of warm and cool colours.*

25

PROJECTS

PLANT ON A WINDOWSILL

▲ **1** *It was a gloomy day, but nevertheless the space beyond the window was relatively light. Notice how soft and diffuse the cast shadow is and how dark and rich the tones within the plant form are.*

People who are new to painting are often lost for something to paint. Far too often they resort to working from photographs. There is nothing inherently wrong with using photographs as reference. The problem is that inexperienced artists copy photographs slavishly and don't involve themselves with the process of composition. They also lose an opportunity to improve their powers of observation, of seeing at firsthand how light and colour can change from one minute to the next and alter the appearance of things. It is remarkably easy to find subjects to paint from life and the process will be immensely rewarding and enjoyable.

A still-life group is easily assembled and can be lit in different ways. You can do some of the 'composing' before you put pencil to paper, arranging the object to make an interesting composition.

The artist, Francis Bowyer, selected a potted plant and placed it on a windowledge so that there was light behind it. It was an overcast day, the light was subdued and the contrasts of light and dark were soft.

Francis used a primarily wet-in-wet technique, laying in washes of wet paint, flowing one colour into another, searching for the image. His paintings are explorations. He applies paint, takes it off, applies more – changing, adjusting and making assessments at each stage. He contemplates the painting, so that he can decide 'where it needs to go'. To the onlooker it might seem uncontrolled, even risky, but Francis is very aware of what he is doing; he describes painting pictures as 'living in hope, but with a desperate fear that I am going to fail'.

His work looks 'painterly', glowing with rich colours and build-ups of texture, but it is deeply rooted in drawing. His profound understanding of form and and his awareness of spatial relationships give his work integrity and conviction.

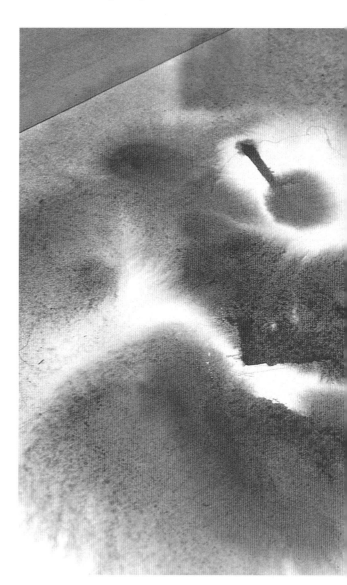

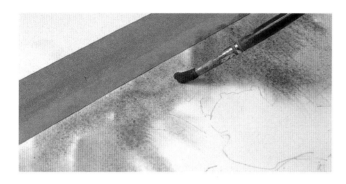

▲ 2 *The artist started by wetting the paper (Arches Not surface). He then flooded in colour – olive green, Indian red and Winsor violet.*

▼ 3 *Still working wet-in-wet, he floods in a mixture of Indian red and alizarin crimson, to stand effectively for the plant form.*

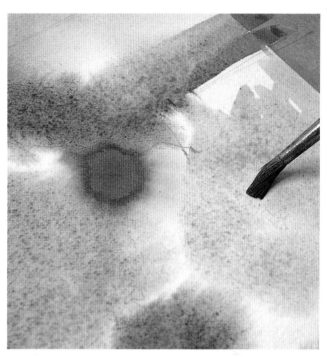

▲ 4 *More colour is added to the wet paint surface – cobalt green for the leafy areas and a pale wash of Winsor violet for the surface of the windowsill.*

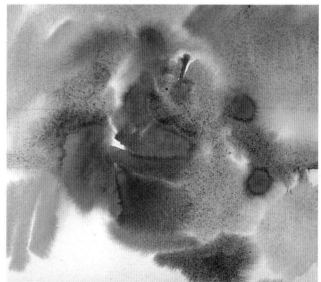

▲ 5 *The subject is very loosely established, the broad forms shimmering on the paper surface. As you can see, parts of the paper surface are dry and others are still wet.*

▶ **6** *Francis likes to work wet-in-wet. Here he rewets the surface by spraying it with water. The water droplets cause the paint to granulate in some areas.*

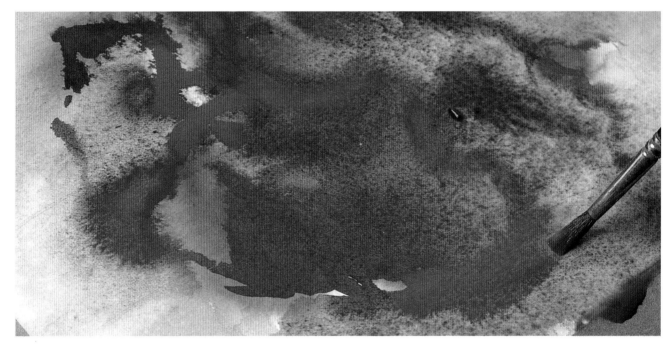

▲ **7** *More colour is flooded in, this time a rich opaque cadmium red. Study the subject carefully, looking for the light and dark tones, for the broad forms, for relationships.*

◀ **8** *The artist rewets the surface again because he is still working very freely. Here he uses his finger to work into the paint surface.*

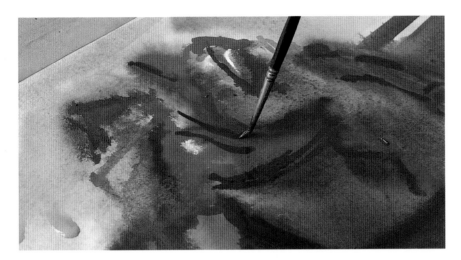

◀ 9 *At this stage the artist begins to add more detail, bringing the image into tighter focus. With a small brush he uses blue paint and a cool red to 'draw' details such as the veining on the leaves and the stems of the leaves. Never stop studying the subject and don't be afraid to redraw and correct inaccuracies or make adjustments that will give you a better image.*

▲ 10 *Here the artist is using opaque paint, adding more layers to create a highly complex picture surface.*

▶ 11 *Here you can see the way in which the picture has emerged as if by magic from the support.*

▶ **12** *At this stage the artist decided to rework the picture. He wet the paper and lifted colour with a sponge, thereby creating a veil of subtle colour.*

▼ **13** *Here he takes more colour off with a wet brush.*

◀ 14 *More colour is flooded in to refine the forms and add further variations of texture. This is done after Francis has spent some time contemplating the picture.*

▼ 15 *The final image has a glorious shimmering quality, with colour and form constantly shifting to create a lively image. The artist has worked with the subject but has allowed the paint and the paint surface to talk back to him, confident that he can keep in balance the demands both subject and materials make. It's a risky process but the result is an exciting image.*

TECHNIQUES

COMPOSING WITH LIGHT

Composition is the process by which an designs or constructs a picture. If a picture hold the viewer's attention and communicate, there must be a logical relationship between the pictorial image and the flat area it occupies.

The artist must 'make a picture', using the shapes and colours in the subject, manipulating, selecting, editing and emphasizing to create an image that is effective and unique. All these elements must be juggled and refined so that they work in relation to one another and to the four edges of the image.

Sarah Holliday, whose work is reproduced on this page, is fascinated by light and the ambiguities created by reflected images. She works with still life because the subjects are accessible and easily manipulated, and offer endless variations. She particularly enjoys 'balancing abstract and figurative elements within a composition, adding a sort of dynamic tension to the whole thing'. And, as she points out, still-life subjects often contain very basic abstract shapes, such as the circle of an apple.

In her compositions she usually combines plant forms with geometric shapes, playing the natural and organic qualities of the one against the more formal qualities of the other.

She works entirely from drawings, which allows her to focus on the subject without distraction. She draws the essentials: the precise location of the sunlight, which can change very quickly; the distribution of light and shade; and all the features that excite her. Details like the veining of leaves can be studied later.

◄ *'Begonia 1' by Sarah Holliday. The stick in the left hand pot and the shadow of the mirror on the right create strong vertical divisions. The mirror and its shadow provide two bold squares: the mirror is a square of light counterpointed by the dark square of its reflection.*

By placing pots and apples in a line across the picture area, the artist actually reduces the sense of space, emphasizing the abstract, pattern-making qualities of the image. The leaves and their reflection form a colourful diagonal. By merging shadows and objects, the artist draws attention to the intervals of light between them. The halo of backlighting adds atmosphere.

◀ *'Spider Plant' by Sarah Holliday. In this study the artist has created an image from a spider plant and a dramatically lit mirror. To produce this striking image the artist has made some slight modifications to the arrangement, moving things slightly, refining something here, leaving some elements out there, to maximize impact.*

For example, there was a little metal dog in the group; she left the ornament out of the image, but retained the shadows thrown by its legs because they contributed a useful shape to the composition. The pot has been played down because it was not an interesting shape, though the reflections are. The dark wedge shape behind the mirror balances a similar shape on the left-hand side, anchoring the whole picture and at the same time giving a clue to the presence of the mirror.

The initial stimulus and drawings are just the start; next comes 'the really exciting stage – working out the composition'. She makes a working drawing, again tonal, to establish the composition, refine the shapes, looking for repeats and relationships, and wrestles with the tonal values.

She thinks that the main problem people have is failing to consider the picture as a whole. You should try to think of your picture as a rectangle covered with different shapes and patches of colour that can be manipulated to suit your needs. The picture plane can be divided up in pleasing ways, and shapes can be refined so that they have a relationship with each other.

33

Light reveals form

ONE OF THE enthralling and confusing aspects of light is the way it both reveals the world to us but at the same time plays tricks, concealing, confusing and always beguiling us.

In the search for 'reality', which has consumed much of Western art since the Renaissance, the artist has been concerned with using the distribution of light and dark around an object to reveal and describe its volume and form, to create an illusion of three dimensions on a two-dimensional surface. But we don't see the world as a series of snapshots. Our field of vision is precisely focused at the centre and blurred at the periphery. Our eyes dart about, taking in bits of information here and there, processing and extrapolating to make sense of what we see. So a painting in which everything is rendered with equal clarity will appear less 'real' than one which is apparently more ambiguous.

The constant shifts of natural light complicate the process further. Distant hills that seem solid, monumental and almost close to at one moment can appear diffuse and insubstantial, mere wisps of things, at another.

'Figure in Light' by Stan Smith. Light streaming through a window here illuminates and defines the figure and at the same time dissolves it into abstract shapes. The artist has exploited these ambiguities: in some places the figure is seen as light flesh set against a dark background; in others it is seen as dark against light.

35

PROJECTS

EGGS IN A CONTAINER

Why waste time looking for 'exciting' subjects when there are marvellous things in the fridge or larder. The artist, Stan Smith had been given a gift of assorted ducks', guinea fowls' and hens' eggs. The simplicity of the forms, the delicacy of the colours and the brittleness of the shells cried out to be painted.

Light from a nearby window washed across the forms, creating patterns of light and dark, emphasizing the contrast between the smooth, fragile surfaces of the eggs and the dimpled texture of the cardboard carton.

A box of hens' eggs will do just as well, but try to find a cardboard container as the polystyrene versions have a less interesting texture and colour. Several eggs in a china dish or a wicker basket would also make a pleasing study.

Simplicity is the key to this project so spend time contemplating the group before you start. If a natural light source is not conveniently available, use a table lamp or a candle to create a strong directional light, which will emphasize the pleasing shapes and textures.

Start by making a quick tonal study of the subject in pencil. This will help you to analyse the subject and fix it in your mind. Think carefully about the way you intend to proceed; use only a few colours and keep the washes to a minimum. Having planned the painting, work as quickly as you can. Don't rework it. If you aren't satisfied with your first efforts, do it again . . . and again. The great advantage of a still-life group is that you can come back to it.

▲ 1 *The subject is eggs in a carton. We happened to have ducks', guinea fowls' and hens' eggs, but hens' eggs alone will do just as well. The artist was captivated by their wonderfully subtle colours, their compact forms and the contrast between their smooth shells and the soft, pitted paper surface of their container. The group provides a subtly coloured subject in primarily neutral shades. Notice the way the light falls around the forms, creating interesting patterns, as well as giving us clues about their shapes and volume.*

▲ 2 *The artist worked on a smoothish paper – Cotman with a Not surface. He started by toning the paper with a wash of raw sienna to give the paper a warm, virtually transparent glow. To do this he mixed the wash and then laid it on briskly with a sponge.*

▶ **3** *When the paper was dry he started to lay in the broad outlines of the form, working directly with a No. 6 brush. Don't hesitate. Study the subject and then draw what you see, allowing the brush to 'feel' its way about the forms. Look at the subject rather than the image; really concentrate and be bold. If you find your drawing is inaccurate, you can make adjustments as you paint, and the overpainted marks will become part of the final image. Don't forget that watercolour dries much lighter than it looks when wet, so these apparently bold marks will be much less bold when dry.*

The artist laid in areas of tone at an early stage using thin washes – here of cadmium yellow pale.

◀ **4** *The artist is working with washes of chrome, cadmium yellow, burnt sienna and Payne's grey. He applies the washes wet-in-wet, allowing one colour to melt into another to achieve subtle gradations that cannot be achieved in any other way. Notice how he has painted the spaces between the eggs – the negatives rather than the positives. This is an excellent way of achieving an accurate drawing and also allows him to minimize the painting of the eggs; he wants to keep the paint in these areas as fresh and transparent as possible. Too much overworking to get the drawing right would detract from the delicacy of the surface, which is the main characteristic of the subject.*

◀ **5** *The image is emerging from the washes of subtle colour. Notice the way crisp edges define the junction between light and dark on the angular forms of the container and the more gradual and blurred transitions on the curving surface of the eggs.*

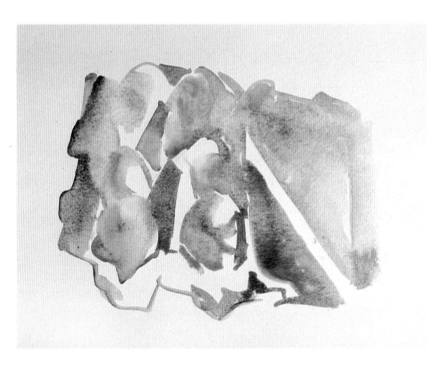

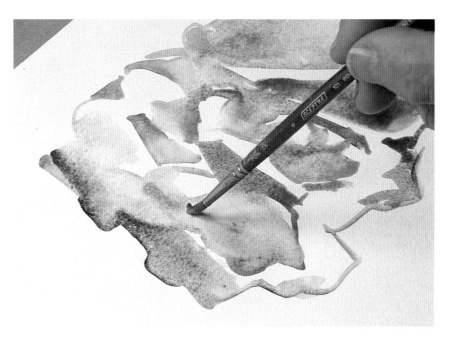

◀ 6 *Working wet-in-wet, the artist touches in warm yellow highlights.*

▼ 7 *The brightest tones and the mid-tones have been established. Now the artist lays in the darkest tones in the recesses of the container. He uses Payne's grey, loading a No. 6 brush and touching in the colour with the very tip. It bleeds into the surrounding still-wet paint to create precise yet soft-edged dark tones.*

◀ **8** *The artist continues to work into the image, adding more dark and mid-tones, but keeping the washes fresh and clear. He doesn't scrub the paint. He constantly refers back to the subject, making adjustments as the light changes.*

▼ **9** *The final image combines careful observation, respect for the special qualities of the subject and a controlled use of the medium. Much of the work was done working wet-in-wet, but further fresh layers have then been applied. The paint surface is clear and lucid. The artist used a limited palette.*

39

LIGHT ON THE FIGURE

When we talk of the figure in art we are dealing with a big subject that includes portraits, single-figure studies, groups, draped figures and nudes, figures in action and figures in an interior. There are two important ways of studying what light can do to the human form. You can look at the work of other artists, both contemporary and from the past, in galleries and in reproduction. These will give you clues and ideas for your own work.

By far the most important way of finding out about the figure in light, however, is direct observation and sketching. If you have friends or family who are interested, you may be able to persuade them to sit for you, but in the end you will undoubtedly be your own most amenable sitter. This, together with the cost of hiring models, explains why self-portraits feature so regularly in artists' work. Life classes at local colleges offer excellent opportunities to work from the nude at very little cost. If you have a group of friends interested in painting, you could even hire a model of your own, sharing the cost among you. A local school or art college would be able to give you a list of life models.

▼ *Here two figures are caught in light streaming in from a window. This composition flouts the traditional rules in that the two figures are, in fact, more or less symmetrically placed and because both gaze out of the composition. Notice the way the eye tends to dance from one pool of light to another, so that the two figures seem to be trapped in light.*

▲ *The light from the open windows falls across the reclining figure, illuminating the back and upper thigh, catching the side of the left hand and parts of the face. This is a perfect demonstration of the shadows being used to explain the solids; sometimes the shadows become almost solid things in their own right. In some places you read dark lines on the light, in others you read the light out of the dark. The front of the figure is in its own shadow, the dark tones visually linking it with the interior space. Notice the almost abstract shapes defined by the highlighted areas.*

On these pages I have shown several studies by Stan Smith, an artist who works primarily with the figure. His large oils are very often concerned with the way light dissolves and resolves forms, but these direct studies are the raw material from which he works up his ideas.

Get into the habit of keeping a sketchbook and in just the same way as you note forms and colours, also focus on the way that light affects the subject – not just its structural appearance but also its mood. Jot down special light effects, noting the source, direction, intensity and colour of the light. Supplement your drawing and colour notes with annotations – anything that will help recall the details to mind.

▲ Here we have an example of the inside/outside theme – a subject full of ambiguity and one to which many artists constantly return. A figure is framed in a doorway. The brilliance of the sunlight outside is contrasted with the cool, grey light indoors. The figure is cropped by the doorway, so that we have a sense of someone glimpsed and caught unawares, giving the painting a sense of intimacy.

◄ In this study a single figure is seen against the light and casts a shadow on the wall. Notice the way the artist has seen the back of the figure and the cast shadow as a single complex shape; in fact the shadow has more significance than the subject. Notice also the interesting shapes trapped between the figure and its shadow.

41

TECHNIQUES

LIGHT ON FLESH

In sympathetic hands watercolour has a transparency, delicacy and lightness of touch that is unmatched by any other medium. It can also be used in a direct, punchy way to produce gloriously bold and colourful images. To get the best from it you must match your approach to the subject.

Figure painting requires a feeling for the bulk and solidity of forms, as well as an understanding of the subtleties of the skin which covers those forms. Poor drawing and heavily handled paint result in figures that are flabby and unconvincing, with flesh that is dull and dead.

The white of the paper under transparent washes gives watercolour its special liveliness and translucency. But the white of the paper can also contribute to the image in other ways. In this study of a nude in a sunlit room, the white of the paper stands for the colour of the flesh in light, the fine muslin curtain and the sunlight dappling the patterned wall behind the figure. In many ways the white of the paper can be seen as light.

You can give a watercolour painting a definite mood by toning the white paper with a very pale wash. The early watercolourists did this in their topographical work, using Naples yellow in summer to give the painting warmth and Payne's grey in winter to give it a cool cast. If you look back at the painting of 'Eggs' on pages 36–9, you'll find that by toning the paper with Naples yellow the artist gave the painting a delicate, sunny feeling.

◀ 1 *In this detail you can see how the white of the paper has been allowed to stand for the brightest flesh tones – all the light areas of the flesh are either white or a conditioned white. Elsewhere transparent washes of earth reds and browns applied wet-in-wet describe the warm flesh mid-tones. Over this the artist has applied transparent watercolour and body colour wet-on-dry, creating crisply defined patterns of colour which capture the patterns of the shadows cast by the tracery of the balcony. It is the crispness of these edges and the sharp contrast of tone that give us a clue to the quality of the light.*

▶ 2 *This study was made from life. The artist, Stan Smith, wanted to capture the quality of the light shining through a typically ornate Parisian balcony and being filtered by fine muslin curtains. We will look at the way in which the sense of brilliant but modified light has been achieved.*

TECHNIQUES

LIGHT ON WALLPAPER

The room was furnished with a rather lush wallpaper with a repeat floral pattern. The artist was interested in the way light fell on the wallpaper, bleaching it, so that it contrasted with the rich colours in the shadow areas. Painting patterns, fabrics and furnishings often presents the beginner with a problem. There is a tendency to render the pattern precisely, but if you do this the pattern will become too important and will leap out of the picture, drawing attention away from other important elements. Here the artist has summarized the paper so that it appears rich but not overwhelming.

▲ 1 *A wash of very dilute terre vert and burnt sienna is used to wash in the wallpaper colour where it is away from the direct light. A crisp edge defines the edge of the shadowed area. A cool mixed blue-grey is added wet-in-wet to re-create the dappling of the surface.*

▼ 2 *With the tip of a No. 6 brush and the same blue-grey mix, the artist touches in a summary of the floral pattern. He is creating an 'impression' of the motif, as it would be experienced by someone in the room, not a detailed record for a student of wallpaper design.*

▶ **3** *While the motifs are still wet, he blots those that are in full sunlight, to blur and bleach them.*

▼ **4** *The artist has created the illusion of light falling on a single surface which is seen in both light and shadow. In the shadow areas the richness and texture of the wallpaper is apparent; in the sunlit areas it is bleached out.*

TECHNIQUES

LIGHT THROUGH MUSLIN

▼ *2 A flowing line captures the character of the main border decoration. There is no single correct way of painting any subject; artists are always searching for a means of describing what they see, an approximation that will work in the context.*

The way Stan Smith approaches these descriptions of light is very simple indeed, though it takes practice, confidence and skill to know just how much or how little to do. In places he uses very little paint; calligraphic marks describe and follow forms, a splash of light is hinted at by the contrasts or shadows that define it, and what is left out is as important as what he chooses to put in.

Watercolour allows you to say a great deal with very little, but you do have to plan to get it right. Here he has used the white of the paper and the transparency of the paint to create the illusion of a diaphanous fabric fluttering in the breeze from an open window. For the beginner it takes an enormous leap of faith to believe that you can do so little and imply so much.

▲ *1 Use a thin mix of Payne's grey to paint the pattern on the muslin curtains. Work freely, to achieve the broken and irregular quality of the pattern as it is modified by the folds of the fabric. Here the artist uses a twisting movement with the flat of the brush to create a continuous line that changes in width.*

▶ *3 From the patches of white paper on the girl's face, and the way the white paper in the area of the window opening is broken up, we deduce that we are seeing light coming through a muslin curtain. When you study the picture in detail you will see that there are very few clues, but those that are given are very effective indeed. The artist has exploited the transparency of the watercolour, the crispness of edges and the white of the paper with a deftness of touch that comes from a lifetime of looking and exploring.*

47

TECHNIQUES

DRAMATIC LIGHT

In this dramatic image light is very much the subject of the painting. It is a heightened, theatrical light, splashing down like a spot from above. Stan Smith is interested in the paradox of light as a transitory phenomenon and light as a constant. 'We tend to think of light as constantly changing, but although the light might be in this position at least ten times a year, the figure won't be there again,' he says.

The composition is based on a strong diagonal occupying the lower half of the picture plane.

The sitter was captured in the light cast through a Venetian blind. All the forms are picked out very simply by light overlaid on the flesh colour. The figure is loosely described in warm earth tones – burnt sienna, raw umber and yellow ochre – with Naples yellow for the light. Notice the way the bands of light are seen as a warm buttery colour as they illuminate the flesh tones, and a cool blue as they fall across the blue carpet. The insubstantial background focuses attention on the figure, rendered in a neutral mix of Payne's grey and cobalt blue. 'The background mustn't be dead,' Stan says. 'It must have tonal value. But it must also have colour value. Something with a little bit of the complementary will give it zest. Here the orangy flesh tones are enlivened by the complementary blues in the background.'

The artist used a combination of gouache and body colour (opaque forms of watercolour) on a warm neutral paper.

▶ **1** *In this dramatic study of a figure, light is the real subject of the painting. The artist has simplified the bands of light to create a dramatic effect. I was interested in the way the bands of paint had been applied, as the precision of the mark didn't look like the mark of a brush. I asked the artist, Stan Smith, to re-create the process for me.*

▼ **2** *The flesh tones were laid in simply in warm earth colours. The artist then cut narrow strips of paper, the width of the required mark, and loaded them with paint.*

▼ **3** *The paint-covered strip was then touched on to the figure to create a band of colour.*

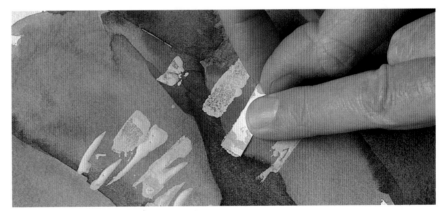

▼ **4** *The mark left has an interesting quality: crisp edges and an uneven paint application that combines the qualities of controlled and accidental marks.*

Light in interiors

M OST OF US spend much of our time indoors, in our home or office, or in public spaces like shops, banks or museums, so the interior provides an obvious and available theme for the artist.

The interior space is an enclosed composition. The space is defined and contained, so the artist can ensure that the viewer's eye is held within the picture area. The subject has an inherent completeness.

Studies of interiors generally have a revealing and intimate quality, providing an evocative glimpse of domestic spaces and everyday objects, of someone else's life. Still-life or figure groups are often included, sometimes providing an important focus, often as an incidental part of a complex whole.

Your own home will provide you with a rich source of subjects – the cluttered corner of a living room, a hallway with discarded coats and boots, or a bedroom glimpsed through a half-opened door. Subjects such as these recur time and time again in the work of artists like Pierre Bonnard (1867–1947), Gwen John (1876–1939) and Edouard Vuillard (1868–1940).

'Interior with Bottle and Flowers'
by Sophie Knight. There is a
marvellous sense of filtered light in
an enclosed, interior space in this
luminous and atmospheric painting.
The artist used a combination of
watercolour and body colour,
building up layers of transparent
and semitransparent colour for
the golden background. These
insubstantial paint layers are
contrasted with the touches of
bright opaque colour – on the
flowers and on the objects on the
table. The brilliant blue of the
tablecloth is complemented by the
touch of bright orange on the label
on the bottle.

NATURAL OR ARTIFICIAL LIGHT?

Light is often the real subject of an interior study, establishing a mood, holding disparate elements together, emphasizing forms here, rendering them ambiguous there.

Natural light streaming in through a window or an open door introduces a sense of 'outside' and the open spaces beyond the enclosed interior. Sometimes the light source is seen and a view through a window or a door gives us a glimpse of landscape or garden – another world. Traditionally the light source was often placed beyond the picture area, so that observed light and shadow are the only clues to its existence.

Artificial light sources emphasize the contained or even claustrophobic nature of the interior and can be used to spotlight some areas, creating mysterious pools of darkness elsewhere. It is more intimate and concealing, and because it belongs in that space it has a more self-contained quality.

There are many different artificial light sources, each with a different mood and colour. A single incandescent light bulb casts a bleak, pitiless light with harsh, often strange shadows. A gleaming brass candelabrum suggests magnificence, while table lamps and standard lamps create pools of intimate light throughout the space, with mysterious shadows between. In our homes light is used quite consciously to create mood. We have direct light to work by, but wall lights and table lamps are used to create atmospheric background lighting. Romantic dinners are candlelit, and firelight has such an evocative appeal that fake fires fuelled by gas are common in homes in smoke-free zones.

Artists prefer natural light because all artificial light distorts colour to a greater or lesser degree. Natural light can be modified by blocking it with drapes or filtering it through gauzy fabrics or Venetian blinds. Stan Smith's paintings on pages 35, 43 and 48 all deal with the human figure seen

in an interior illuminated by modified natural light.

Artificial light is controlled light. It can be turned on or off, raised or lowered, directed on to the subject or bounced off an adjacent surface. A shaded light creates an area of direct, bright illumination, but a more diffuse light generally percolates through the shade, bathing adjacent

objects in a soft and often coloured glow that gives the group a harmonious unity. An Anglepoise or a spotlight can be used to create a dynamic directional light. Light can be used to distort forms so that they become strange. For example, as a child you may have put a torch under your chin so that your face was lit from below; the effect is quite disturbing.

▲ *'Still Life Session at the Seed Warehouse' by Trevor Chamberlain. Still life groups can generally be arranged so you can 'compose' the subject itself as well as on the support. Light is a very important element – here the painters have a desk lamp directed onto the subject. The light is being thrown from the side to give a variety of interesting shadows.*

53

PROJECTS

ARTICHOKE FLOWER

A single flower in a bottle provides the motif for this painting. It is a simple subject, but with a little thought Stan Smith has made something beautiful and intriguing of it.

In a very shallow picture plane the painting establishes an inside/outside theme, with light passing through the window and picking out the flower head. This is enhanced by the contrast between the dimly lit and muted interior space and the brightly lit exterior. Notice the way the strip of the window reveal takes the full force of the light, providing a particularly sharp contrast between one area and another.

Out of the window we can see a chimney, which appears almost the same size as the plant, though in fact it is much larger. This introduces an element of ambiguity and tension. The rich warm oranges of the chimneypots pick up the golden ochre of the flower head, providing a visual link, on a diagonal that runs from corner to corner of the image.

To capture the crisp transitions between light and dark the artist masked the areas, using masking tape and masking fluid. Masking is an extremely useful technique that allows you to flood colour on, keeping it loose and free, overlaying and letting one colour melt into another. If the colour looks as though it is going to run away from you, it can be arrested by drying it with a hair-dryer. Then at the very end you can remove the mask to reveal crisp white paper. The white paper can be left as highlight or local colour (daisies, for example), or it can be washed with bright, pure colour to create a brilliant focal point, as the artist did with the golden flower head. Because masking is so effective, there is a temptation to overdo it, so that it becomes a cliché. In the project on page 70 the artist has reserved many areas of crisp white or pale tones without using any masking technique.

▲ **1** *A deceptively simple subject – an artichoke flower in a bottle, on a windowsill – provides the artist with a stimulating subject.*

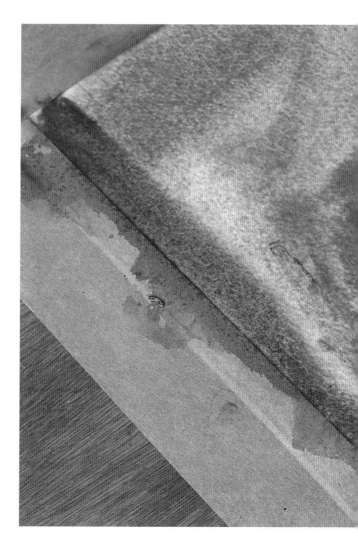

▲ **2** *The artist worked on a sheet of Saunders Waterford watercolour paper with a rough surface. He drew in the broad outlines of the subject with an HB pencil. He wanted to capture the way the flower catches the light. To reserve the paper so that he could judge the correct tone at the last minute, he masked it with colourless masking fluid.*

▲ **3** *The other bright area in the subject was the inside of the window reveal. He could have masked this with fluid, but it was a large area and he wanted a neat 'architectural' edge. Masking tape was used here and is an ideal solution. This is a low-tack tape, available from art and graphics shops. He laid it down and trimmed it off with a craft knife.*

◄ **4** *Colour is washed on – Prussian blue with a touch of alizarin, crimson and raw umber – applied wet-in-wet. You can wash the colour right over the masked areas.*

▼ **5** *The chimney is laid in with Indian red.*

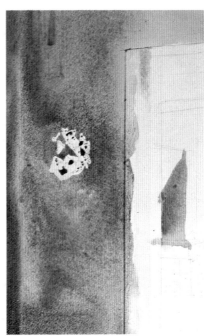

► 6 *The area beyond the window was washed in with ultramarine. Then the artist drew the bottle in thinned black with just a little ultramarine. Using the same mix, he then drew in the linear details around the window. He used a ruler to guide him. To do this, hold the ruler on its side and use it as a guide for your hand. If you rule against the ruler itself, you risk paint getting under it.*

► 7 *Masking fluid can be removed by rubbing it gently with your finger; it comes away as a rubbery film. This must be done when the paint is dry.*

▼ 8 *Next the masking tape is removed.*

▲ **9** *The colours of the flower head can now be washed in on the fresh white paper. The artist used cadmium yellow deep for the top side and Indian red with a touch of ultramarine for the lower petals.*

▼ **10** *A few more lines are drawn in using the ruler, in ultramarine with a touch of black.*

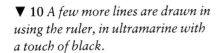

▲ **11** *In the final image there is a harmony of warm and cool colours. The vertical support mirrors the vertical nature of the flower and the chimney.*

CHILD CONTRE-JOUR

The figure *contre-jour*, or against the light, has long been popular with artists. By placing the figure in partial silhouette, the image is bathed with a diffuse, mysterious light. The viewer is given some information, but much of the image is implied and ambiguous. If the figure is placed against a very bright light, the result will be harsher and more dramatic – with more contrast between the light and dark areas. To achieve a true *contre-jour* effect, you may need to filter the light by draping muslin or some other fine fabric over the window.

The figure in an interior has been a common theme throughout art history. As soon as a figure is introduced, it tends to become the focal point, no matter how small or sketchily defined. The child was caught in profile just as she got up from the table. The moment is transitory, the movement out of the picture space implicit in her stance. She is trapped in light and rendered timeless on the picture surface.

Francis Bowyer treats the figure and her surroundings as a pattern of light and dark, with diffuse light defining forms, echoing tones and colour, and melding the whole into a single coherent entity.

▲ 2 *The artist has flooded the paper with water and lays in the broad forms of the subject using sap green, ultramarine, yellow ochre and alizarin crimson.*

▼ 3 *You can see the way in which the wet-in-wet application causes the forms to dissolve, creating ghostly images. It takes great confidence to work in this way. By applying the paint boldly with a loaded brush or by allowing it to bleed off the brush, the artist keeps the paint fresh. Avoid the temptation to overwork the surface or scrub one colour into another.*

▲ 1 *The child was captured as she rose to leave the table – a movement caught in time. The artist made a sketch on the spot and then worked the image up in his studio. We have re-created the event to give you an idea of what he was working with and what he made of it.*

◀ **4** *The subject is very broadly established, but it has been carefully observed. The artist works fast and with great intensity, then breaks off to spend some time contemplating the image.*

▼ **5** *More washes of pure colour are added – cool blues for the figure, which is cast into shadow, and warm, rich colours for the drapery about the window, where it catches the light.*

◀ **6** *The artist drops a pair of L-shaped masks around the image. This helps him 'see' how the composition is working. He also experiments with cropping the image, to see if it might look more effective as as a square rather than a rectangle, for example.*

▼ **7** *Here he saturates the paper with water so that he can apply more colour wet-in-wet.*

▶ **8** *The image is clearly established – it is figurative, with abstract qualities. These are evident in the way the artist interprets light as patches of pure colour.*

▲ **9** *The artist wanted to achieve a particular mood in the picture and having contemplated it, he added more paint layers, some opaque, some transparent. The final image is descriptive and entertaining, a symphony of light and dark and patches of colour.*

PROJECTS

CANDLELIGHT 1

Candles produce a soft, flickering light that gives the most mundane setting an aura of mystery and romance. The flame has a brilliant, pulsating intensity, while a halo of illumination spreads out from the centre, creating an envelope of hazy, shifting light. Candlelight has a luminous quality, with subtle gradations of tone rather than the harsh contrasts of incandescent light. To show luminosity you need a fairly limited palette and muted colours.

In our studies the candle is placed within the picture area. The flame is the lightest area in the picture; everything else is darker in tone. Colours are subtly shaded and graded from the flame out to the concluding darkness. Find a way to soften the edges of each gradation so that it blends into the adjacent area.

Adrian Smith tried two different approaches to the image. In the first he worked up the tones in charcoal, fixing them and then washing colour over the tonal study. The combination of charcoal and fixative gave the paper an absorbent quality, with the watercolour tending to seep and bleed, creating a softly blurred effect that suited the subject.

▲ **2** *The artist started by blocking in the dark areas using a charcoal stick. In some areas he used it on its side to block in broad areas of tone. Here he uses a soft putty eraser to pull out areas of highlight.*

▼ **3** *When the artist has established the lights and darks to his satisfaction he fixes the drawing. This prevents the charcoal powder from contaminating the watercolour.*

▲ **1** *This is the subject, but not precisely as the artist saw it. He worked without any background light at all; the photographer, on the other hand, used a flash.*

▲ 4 *Using a mix of ultramarine, cobalt and Payne's grey, he washes in the background. The paper has become very absorbent – a bit like blotting paper.*

▲ 5 *He uses a mix of indigo and raw sienna for the darker tones, letting the colours run and blend. Here he uses a wet sponge to lift off colour around the halo of the flame to heighten the effect.*

▶ 6 *He uses the indigo–raw sienna mix to lay in the dark side of the fruit dish. The light and dark tones have now been established.*

▶ 7 *He next touches in local colour, primarily in the illuminated areas, where the light allows the colour to be seen.*

▲ 8 *The rough texture of the paper combines with the grainy quality of the charcoal underdrawing to create a diffuse aura which captures perfectly the flickering quality of the candle flame.*

◀ 9 *The final image captures the drama of the subject. Now look at the next study of the subject, for which the artist used a different technique.*

PROJECTS

CANDLELIGHT 2

You can learn a lot by returning to the same subject again and again. In this second study of candlelight the artist worked with pure watercolour, building on the experience gained in the first study. Don't think that when you have painted a subject you have finished with it. Each time you will see different aspects of the subject and new solutions will occur to you.

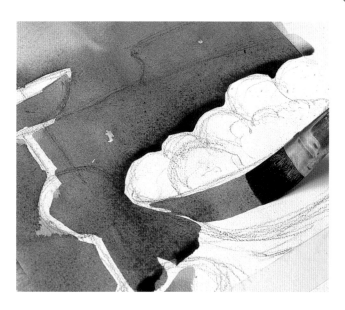

◀ **1** *The artist is painting the same setting as for the previous project.*

▼ **2** *The artist started by first establishing the main elements of the subject in pencil. The drawing should be accurate, but remember that you can make adjustments as you paint. He studied the subject carefully, deciding where exactly the mid-tones lay. He mixed a wash of ultramarine, cobalt and Payne's grey. He used a large wash brush loaded with colour and, working quickly, laid in the first wash.*

▲ **3** *He had mapped the light areas in his mind and as he worked he was careful to leave these clear of paint. Remember that with the use of pure watercolour it is the paper that gives you the lightest tone.*

▼ **4** *He then made a darker colour by adding indigo to his blue-grey mix and laid in the darkest tones in the shadow areas.*

▶ 5 *He uses a broad 'one-stroke' brush to paint the candle stick. He wanted to give the candle a crisp outline to emphasize the strong tonal contrasts. Here the candle is seen against the soft light being bounced against the wall behind.*

▼ 6 *He intensifies the aura of the candle flame by sponging out colour with a damp sponge. Although watercolour has a reputation for being difficult, it is actually quite forgiving. You can lift out colour and make adjustments to a remarkable degree, especially if you use good-quality paper.*

▲ 7 *Here he has laid in the local colours in the fruit dish – orange and green. He then adds darker tones to give the fruits form.*

▶ 8 *In the final image the paint surface is fresh and exciting and the artist has captured the mysterious, shifting quality of the candlelight.*

CHAPTER 5 CHAPTER

Outdoor light

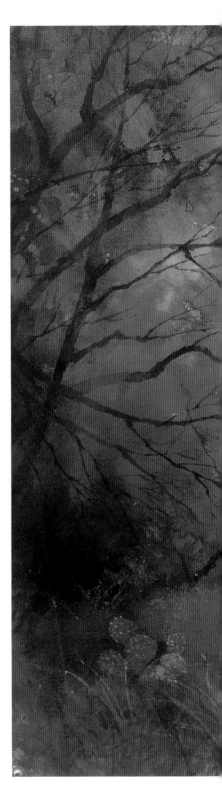

THE APPEARANCE OF the landscape is affected by the quality of the light. This in turn is affected by factors like weather, time of day and even geographical location. The appearance of a landscape can change dramatically from one day to the next, even from minute to minute.

Rain, snow, fog and mist can transform the landscape, and each has its own magic. On a foggy autumnal day only a little weak light manages to struggle through the veil of swirling mist. Water droplets in the air scatter and filter the light, draining colours of their intensity and giving them a bluish cast. Spatial arrangements become confused as tonal contrasts are evened out, forms are flattened and the details of objects appear blurred and indistinct. In such conditions the artist searches for subtle nuances of colour and tone, mixing a range of warm and cool neutrals to create a subdued but atmospheric image.

The same stretch of the countryside will look entirely different on a sunny summer's day. Brilliant sunshine creates contrasts of light and dark, throwing some areas into harsh relief and plunging others into impenetrable shadow. Colours will be seen at their most intense, though on a really dazzlingly bright day they can appear bleached and washed-out.

'*Enchanted Rock, Texas*', *by Shirley Felts. This is an area she returns to time and time again. The heightened colour produced by the threatening storm gives the picture a magical quality.*

TREE ON THE DOWNS

No other medium serves light as well as water-colour. Light is transitory and ambiguous, and in watercolour the white of the paper has some of the same qualities. Just as dark tones and shadows define the bright areas in the subject, so it is only when washes of paint are applied that the paper begins to read as highlight. Stan Smith's treatment of shadow in this study illustrates the point very well.

The stand of trees in its sunny downland location provided an excellent motif for the study of light and shadow. The dark foliage was broken up by a pattern of white branches, boughs and twigs, counterpointed by the tracery of their shadows on the silvery tree trunk. This is a perfect demonstration of how light strikes objects and creates shadows suggesting the dimensions, shape and character of the object on to which they are cast. The highly contrasted lights and darks help to emphasize the brilliance of the day.

All the shadows have a colour value, so don't be tempted to render them in black and white. Create dark tones that have richness by experimenting with mixes – raw umber (a yellowish brown) and Prussian blue (an icy blue) will give you a deep olive, for example. Don't cheat by adding colour to black, because the mixes will be leaden.

The artist used a box of sixteen pan colours with two places to mix colour – the lid and a fold-out palette. He used one brush – a No. 10.

Working quickly, he laid in broad washes of colour, allowing the colours to blend. He left the painting to dry then applied more washes, keeping the image simple and fresh.

You will learn a lot by trying to replicate this painting, but do find opportunities to work directly from nature. Even in a city, there should be a garden or park where you can practise and hone your powers of observation.

▲ 1 *The subject was a tree on a vegetation-covered bank, with summer sun slanting through it. The artist was fascinated by the complex tracery of branches, seen as shadow on the silvery trunk of the tree.*

▼ 2 *Working conditions are not always ideal out of doors, but the artist made do, squatting on the ground to work and replenishing his water jar every now and then from a nearby stream.*

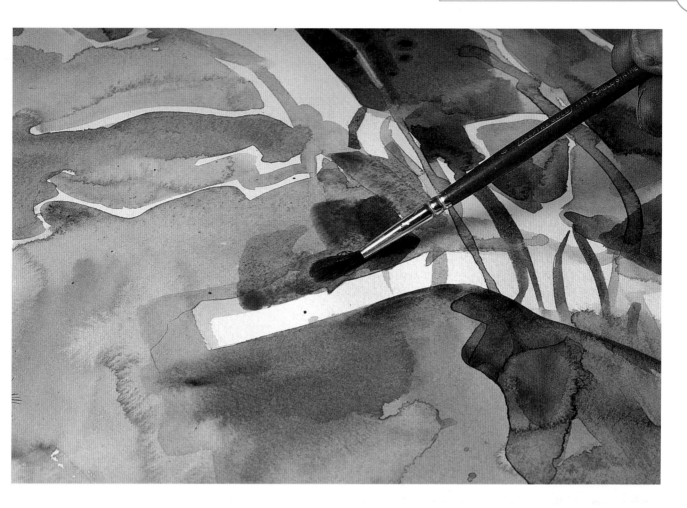

▲ 3 *The artist laid in a wash of greens – sap green, a green mixed from cobalt and cadmium yellow, and a dark green mixed from viridian with raw umber for the dark tones. He didn't have masking fluid so he worked carefully to reserve the white of the paper for the highlighted areas. Crisp edges and sharp contrasts of tone create the effect of maximum brightness.*

Simplify the forms that you see and work boldly. Don't move the paint around too much, otherwise it will soon lose its freshness and look overworked.

▶ 4 *Here you can see the structure of the painting. It is comprised of initial washes and colour added wet-in-wet. More colour was added as the paint surface dried, causing the colours to 'flare' – a happy accident that helps describe the clumpy foliage of trees. Over this he has laid more washes, constantly adjusting his mixes to match the observed colour, but always simplifying, trying to find a direct way of expressing what he sees.*

71

▶ **5** *Darker tones are laid in with ultramarine and darkened green mixes. Cadmium yellow is laid on over the previous washes, now dried in the sun. This warms the areas in the foreground, where the sun warms grass and foliage.*

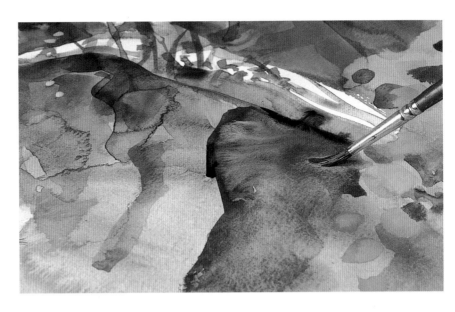

▼ **6** *To capture the intensity and depth of the dark areas in the dense summer foliage, the artist is building up successive layers of transparent colour. This creates dark and mid-tones of great luminosity.*

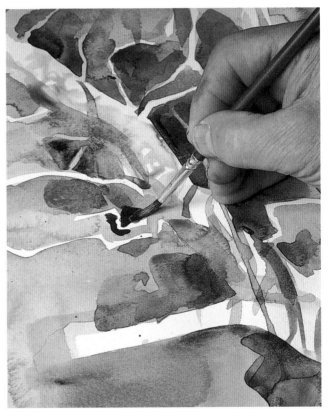

▲ **7** *Here the artist is using the tip of his brush to define some of the branches. He is painting the foliage between, leaving the branches as lighter areas – the negatives rather than the positives.*

▶ **8** *The final image captures the warmth and brightness of the sunny day with great economy. It was painted entirely on location and the artist has successfully captured the mood of the scene.*

LIGHT ON WATER

Water presents the artist with a tantalizing and constantly changing subject. Its most obvious characteristics are its transparency and its reflective qualities, and for this reason water depends for its appearance on the nature of the available light.

Water is a colourless substance, but in large masses it takes on colour from its surroundings. Generally, large bodies of water like the sea and lakes take their colour from the sky, but at the water's edge overhanging trees and adjacent buildings contribute colour.

The sea springs constant surprises, sometimes looking pale and silvery against a dark, lowering sky, and on other occasions looking leaden and solid. In some conditions sea and sky are crisply delineated at the horizon; in others the one melts imperceptibly into the other. Colour, too, varies from a bright blue-green, through the colour of pea soup, to the brown of peaty water.

Water may be moving or static, and this affects its appearance and the way it reflects its surroundings. Not only does water move, it reflects a moving sky. The movement of water creates different shapes on its surface that depend on the nature of the movement. Some of the movements are affected by wind or the wake of a boat. These shapes on

▼ *'Albatross, 1989' by Grahame Sydney. This precisely painted and carefully composed painting has a wonderful sense of tranquillity and timelessness. The slight distortions of the reflection give a clue to the movement on the water's surface.*

the water's surface follow the rules of perspective, becoming smaller in scale as they move away.

Reflections in water are distorted by the ripples that break up the water's surface. The reflecting surface, the water, is always horizontal, and in relatively still water the points of the reflections lie vertically beneath the objects reflected. The per-spective lines of the object and its reflection run to the same vanishing point. Sometimes, however, water and light play visual tricks. Waves can act as a faceted mirror, creating a multiple reflection or appearing to displace it in one direction. As these factors are so difficult to predict direct observation really is the best way to tackle the subject.

◄ *In this study of moored gondolas, by Ian Sidaway, the artist has cropped in to the image to draw attention to the pleasing shapes of the vessels. The rippling water is rendered simply with calligraphic marks that are both descriptive and decorative.*

PROJECTS

VENICE

This painting was developed from a sketch made on location. Albany Wiseman visited Venice quite early in the year. His main concern was to capture the luminous quality of Venetian light, which results from the city's unique combination of big skies over expanses of water. The city often appears insubstantial, a mirage floating on a shimmering surface of water, seen through a gauzy veil of dancing light. Since its foundation, painters have been drawn there, keen to experience its strangely theatrical qualities, impelled to capture an impression of them in paint. So often has the city featured in paintings, drawings, photographs and films that even the first-time visitor has a sense of *déjà vu*.

In this painting the artist depicts that time of day when the city is reduced to a silhouette by the setting sun. The 'cut-out' profiles of rooftops overlap like stage flats, the effects of atmospheric perspective making them appear paler and bluer as they recede into the distance. The artist has focused on this effect, using a limited palette of colours and a series of overlapping washes to describe clusters of buildings. The water, too, is handled with a simple but sure touch. If it were laboured and overworked, it would lack the sparkle inherent in the theme of light on water.

By rigorously editing, selecting and organizing the elements of the composition, the artist has created an image which has a pared-down beauty. And if you study the step-by-step stages, you'll find that he has managed to make the process of painting the picture look deceptively simple too. In fact, the process describes a few easy-to-master techniques which the amateur painter can put to good use in his or her own work. The painting is a fine example of the way that practice and the ability to observe and analyse give an artist the confidence to temper boldness with restraint when appropriate to the subject. You might find it difficult to get started, but it takes years to know just when to leave well alone.

▲ **1** *The painting shows a mist-shrouded sun shining on to the water. The artist used masking fluid to reserve the white paper in those areas where the sun illuminated a path across the water, glancing across the top of the ripples in the water. To create the indistinct image of the sun just behind the church, he wet the paper in that general area. He then laid in the rest of the sky wet-on-dry, using a wash of Naples yellow.*

▲ **2** *He mixed up a colour for water from Prussian green – a dark bluish green – and Winsor blue with a touch of Van Dyke brown.*

▶ **3** *He used tissue to lift out some of the colour from the path of the sun – the sun on the water was so bright it was very light.*

▼ **4** *For the buildings he used Winsor blue with a bit of alizarin crimson and Van Dyke brown, keeping the edges crisp, so that they showed dark against the light sky.*

▲ **5** *He applied a darker tone in the water for contrast.*

◀ **6** *The artist's approach is deceptively simple, but it takes a great deal of practice and a lot of planning to produce such an effective image.*

▲ 7 *A slightly darker tone is applied in the middle distance.*

▼ 8 *Using a dark wash of Payne's grey mixed with Van Dyke brown, the artist starts to put in the poles that emerge from the water. He uses a big brush loaded with paint to give the mark a textural quality.*

◄ **9** *In this detail we see the water before the masking fluid is removed.*

► **10** *Here we can see the way the water sparkles when the masking fluid is removed.*

▼ **11** *The final image captures the mood of the place, the luminous quality of the mist-filtered light and the sparkling, light-scattering quality of the water.*

TECHNIQUES

TIME OF DAY

The character of natural light changes throughout the day, so that bright, early morning light has a very different quality from the glimmering, silvery light of evening. Both colour and the direction and intensity of light and shadows change as the sun rises, passes overhead and then sinks in the west. This means that the same scene can reveal many different appearances, characters and moods in a single day. Weather conditions and seasonal changes increase these potential differences, so that the artist can paint the same scene time and time again and constantly find new themes and motifs.

The Impressionist Claude Monet (1840–1926) explored these changes in his series paintings. The first of these was the 'Haystacks' or 'Grain Stacks' series, painted in the autumn of 1890. He would go out to paint in the early morning or in the hours before sunset, taking paints, easels and several partially completed canvases, often conveying his equipment in a wheelbarrow. He would then work first on one canvas, then on another as the light changed, finding the canvas that most closely resembled the scene in front of him. In this way he was able to record precise shifts of light and tone, and subtle nuances of colour. He was trying 'to convey the weather, the atmosphere and the general mood'. In the 'Grain Stacks' series he also recorded the seasonal changes, capturing the golden colours of autumn, the cold bluish tones of a snowy winter landscape and the fresh pinks and greens of springtime.

Try painting one scene – the view through your window perhaps – in morning, afternoon and evening light, or on a sunny day and in overcast or rainy conditions. Concentrate on the broad forms, the groupings of light and dark, and the colour balances. Watercolour is ideal for making quick notes. Make as many as you can and don't review them until you have several that you can compare and contrast. You will be surprised how very different the results are.

On these pages we show two studies of early morning by different artists. In 'Dawn Mist' by Charles Bartlett, the artist has captured that moment when the rising sun begins to warm and burn up the chilly mists hanging over the marshland. In the second painting John Lidzey describes the same time of day as seen from the window of a north London house. He uses watercolour and Conté pencil, contrasting the orange sky with the complementary blues of the gardens that are still in deep shadow.

PROJECTS

GATEWAY IN TRASIERRA 1

In the following pages Albany Wiseman shows just what a difference a few hours can make to the way a scene is lit, and to the appearance and atmosphere. He has painted two versions of the same scene, one with bright light falling directly on the gateway and the other when the sun has moved, so that the gate is almost backlit. The first was painted in the morning at about ten o'clock; the other was painted a little later.

He worked under a tree that gave a lot of shadow and contrast in the foreground. He drew the wall and the trailing ivy on the left of the picture in some detail, so that the eye is led up and into the painting, and ultimately through the arch that frames the courtyard beyond. This is the focal point of the painting.

He edited out the tree on the right and included a palm tree. Notice also that he cropped the picture. He felt that the weight on the left and right of the composition was too similar. By cropping one side, he gave emphasis to the other and energy to the painting.

Notice that the painting doesn't go right to the edge of the support. This gives the artist the choice of squaring it up at a later date if he wants to, and in many ways this also represents your field of vision more accurately – you don't see a rectangle in precise focus.

◀ ▲ 1 *Two studies of the same scene made on location at Trasierra in Spain. The artist was teaching there and often sat down to paint with his students. The sun was overhead, to the left and slightly behind him, so the sun fell directly on the gateway.*

▶ **2** *The artist worked on an 140lb (300 gsm) Arches Rough surface. He started by laying in the sky, wetting the paper first, then flooding in Winsor blue and dropping in some cerulean blue to create a subtly variegated effect. The sky is critical in a painting and needs to be handled deftly to keep the colour fresh if it is to be convincing. Avoid the temptation to move the colour about once you have put it on. Leave it to dry and you'll be surprised how effective it is.*

▶ **3** *The artist then laid in the foreground with a pale wash of Naples yellow. This is rather a chalky, slightly opaque colour, more like gouache in its characteristics than typical transparent watercolour. Nevertheless, it is a lovely warm yellow, which the artist finds ideal for painting in southern European and Mediterranean locations. He doesn't mix Naples yellow with other colours, because it does render them a bit opaque. Interestingly, when he goes abroad, he sometimes buys colours locally, because the palette he uses in the English climate needs supplementing.*

He was sitting under a tree. The dappled shadows in the foreground were laid in with a mix of Van Dyke brown and a bit of blue. The 'flare' is a bit of accidental mixing that the artist didn't intend but decided to leave.

◀ **4** *He masked the forms of some of the ivy leaves with masking fluid. Do keep an old brush for this purpose and wash it carefully afterwards. When the masking fluid was quite dry, he laid in a loose wash of Hooker's green, which forms the basis of the foliage. He uses Hooker's green with raw sienna for the palm tree, laying in the fronds with a rigger – a brush with long fibres, ideal for linear detail, so-named because it was originally used for laying in the rigging in nautical paintings.*

◀ **5** *For the darker foliage by the gateway the artist used a mix of Hooker's green and Payne's grey. The white of the paper shimmers through the washes of colour and stands for the colour of the sunlit whitewashed wall.*

▼ **6** *The shadows were laid in using a big brush – a No.10. The colour is applied wet-on-dry because the artist wanted a hard line to maximize the contrast between light and dark areas, which enhances the sense of brilliant sunlight. He uses Payne's grey with a little blue. Crisp lines and cool shadow evoke the sense of sunlight.*

▼ **7** *The artist lays in some darker tones for the vegetation, using Hooker's green and Payne's grey. When that is dry he removes the masking fluid by rubbing it gently with a gum eraser (this is made fom Cow Gum adhesive); you can also use your fingertips. Notice how the crisp, masked forms give this area a sparkle and impact.*

◄ **8** *To complete the picture he adds the details within the arch. He used light red for the pantiled roof. This is another colour that is useful in Mediterranean countries. He left the pencil in to convey the detail of the pantiles. When it is dry he adds a little darker tone. He uses the same mix for the terracotta urns: these were old olive-oil vats and are 1.2 metres high. The bright mustard ceramic finials are touched in with a bit of raw sienna. This isn't a particularly bright colour but looks bright against the blue sky.*

GATEWAY IN TRASIERRA 2

This second demonstration is based on a painting made a little later; only an hour or so had passed but the light had changed dramatically. The sun is still on the left but it has moved to eleven o'clock in relation to the artist, so that this side of the gateway is in shadow. Compare the two studies and see how dramatically the passage of the sun has changed the colour and tonal relationships within the subject. You'll also notice that the artist has opted for different compositions, cropping the image to include a tree on the right here, while in the previous picture there is a date palm on the left of the picture.

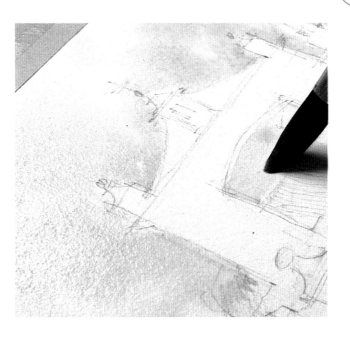

▲ 2 *The artist used an HB pencil for the drawing. He then masked various areas – some of the foliage, the white doves in the yard and the geese – but only the highlight, where they are backlit by the sun. The artist used cerulean blue for the sky in this case. Again it was laid on to wet paper.*

▲ 1 *This is the artist's sketch on which the second demonstration is based. It was painted on location, only an hour or two after the first one, but the light has changed dramatically.*

▲ 3 *The foreground was washed in with Naples yellow, which gives the earth a warm glow. Notice that the artist has used Naples yellow for the underside of the arch. You might expect this area to be dark, but in fact light was reflecting up from the earth below. The wall and gate are painted in cerulean blue with just a touch of Payne's grey.*

85

◀ **4** *The artist then laid in the foliage with a Hooker's green–Payne's grey mix, using the same colour for the shadows. For the dark tones on the geese he uses the Payne's grey-blue mix.*

▼ **5** *He darkened the wall and gate with another wash of colour and, while it was still wet, dropped in a bit of Naples yellow, which gives the wall a warm glow and suggests the effect of light reflecting up from the light-coloured earth.*

◀ **6** *He added more detail to the foliage with the Hooker's green–Payne's grey mix. Payne's grey and Van Dyke brown were used for the dark tones of the gates.*

▼ **7** *The red roof of the yard was washed in with light red, which is qualified by the cool tone beneath. The artist has removed the masking fluid from the ivy-clad wall and washed in sap green, which gives a light but not white highlight to this area. For the tree on the left he uses sap green with a touch of Van Dyke brown to knock it back. He spattered some colour on to the base of the tree to describe the weeds and growth in this area. If you do this, do mask other areas with a sheet of paper to prevent spattered colour from going where it shouldn't.*

TECHNIQUES

WIND, RAIN AND FOG

Inclement weather may not be ideal for personal comfort but it provides the artist with a remarkable range of absorbing and stimulating material. Wind, rain, snow, fog and mist can transform even the most familiar landscapes into something quite fresh and new.

In misty, drizzly weather the landscape is drained of contrasts in colour and tone; it is enveloped in a semi-transparent veil through which details are only fleetingly glimpsed. Sunlight filtered through mist and fog imbues the landscape with a soft, luminous light that has a magical, otherworldly quality. More than any other medium, watercolour allows the artist to achieve a sensation of light and, by carefully mixing washes and flooding one colour into another, create subtle nuances of tone and colour. For misty landscapes you should work primarily wet-in-wet, bleeding one colour into another, blotting and lifting colour to achieve a gauzy, undefined quality. Avoid crisp wet-on-dry brushmarks and hard edges. Details should be applied in dilute colour.

Some of the most dramatic light effects are achieved just before or just after a storm. Often you will find that the sky is extremely dark and brooding in one quarter, while remaining light and bright in another.

It is easiest to study the effects of weather from an indoor location – a window or a doorway which affords a good but protected viewpoint. Cars make

▲ *'On a Sea of Mud, Maldon' by Trevor Chamberlain. In this haunting study of a rainy day on the estuary of the River Blackwater in Essex, the artist has used a limited palette of warm and cool neutrals. The broad form of the image is simply established with a series of wet-in-wet washes, with details laid on to damp paper to give them soft outlines. A few deft touches of crisper colour – on the grounded boat – pull that area into sharper focus.*

◄ *Bill Taylor constantly sketches directly from the landscape, often making several sketches of the same scene. In the vigorous thumbnail sketches shown here, he records the dramatic cloud formations and light effects which announce stormy weather in the mountainous part of the country where he lives. These 'plein-air' sketches are the raw material from which he works up more formal landscape watercolours in the studio.*

excellent mobile studios, and trees or farm buildings may provide temporary shelter and an interesting view. Strong winds are a hazard, but you can stabilize your easel by using a weight or by tethering it to a gatepost or a tree. Artists who spend a lot of time working out of doors soon evolve ingenious devices for making life reasonably comfortable and practical. You'll find that pans of watercolour are easier to handle than tubes, for example.

Weather conditions are generally transitory in our part of the world, so the appearance of the scene may change completely in the space of a few minutes. Work on several studies at the same time, laying in wet washes and moving on to the next study while the first dries. Alternatively, make a series of very quick 'thumbnail' sketches on a single sheet, as Bill Taylor has in the page from his sketchbook shown on the facing page. The English artist J. M. W. Turner (1775–1851) was the master of atmospheric studies of the play of light on landscape and the effects of weather.

TECHNIQUES

MISTS USING 'BLOTESQUE'

'Blotesque' is a technique in which Chinese white is applied under transparent watercolour and then blotted or rubbed back to achieve areas of hazy, softly modulated colour. The technique was devised and used by two painters, Joseph Crawhall (1861–1913) and Arthur Melville (1855–1904). Both were 'Glasgow Boys', members of a loose association of painters based in Glasgow at the end of the nineteenth century. Like the New English Art Club,

founded in 1886, and the Impressionists, the Glasgow school favoured lyrical naturalism and working '*en plein air*'.

Crawhall painted in watercolour and body colour on a fine linen fabric called holland, washing on colour and then blotting it off.

Melville travelled in the Middle East and North Africa, painting in Tangiers and in the desert. In his paintings, highly contrasted light and shadow evince the heat and exoticism of the location.

Melville would often saturate the paper with Chinese white, rinsing off much of the colour so that the paper was impregnated with a thin film of white. He would then make a drawing before applying washes of colour with vigorous brush-strokes, sponging out any superfluous detail. Finally, touches of intense colour would be applied to give the composition life and vibrancy when the paper was nearly dry.

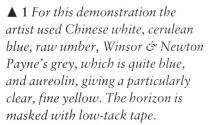

▲ **1** *For this demonstration the artist used Chinese white, cerulean blue, raw umber, Winsor & Newton Payne's grey, which is quite blue, and aureolin, giving a particularly clear, fine yellow. The horizon is masked with low-tack tape.*

He started by laying down Chinese white and a touch of cerulean blue and aureolin, rubbing some pure Chinese white in the wet colour. He was careful to take the colour right down to the horizon line, then evened it out a little with a dry brush.

◄ **2** *With a dry sponge he lifts some of the paint, creating a softly defined cloud in the sky.*

▼ ◄ **3** *He used a mix of cerulean blue and Payne's grey to lay in the line of hills. Using a tissue, he lifts off some of the colour to create a soft and hazy effect.*

▼ **4** *Next he laid in another wash of the cerulean blue/Payne's grey mix to intensify the form of the hills.*

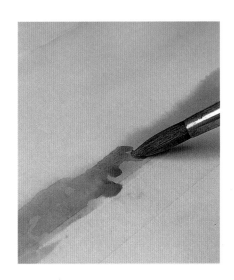

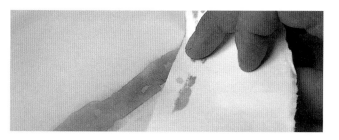

◄ **5** *When the paint has begun to go off but is still damp in places, he used blotting paper to take off some of the colour. This creates areas of misty, diffuse colour.*

◄ **6** *He laid in another loose wash of colour, this time a slightly warmer mix of raw umber and cerulean blue, blotting it as he did with the previous washes.*

Finally he draws in the shoreline with a mix of Payne's grey and raw umber. The line is drawn freehand; notice how he uses his little finger as a support to keep his hand perfectly steady.

◄ **7** *The masking tape is removed, revealing the crisp edge of the shoreline.*

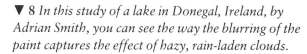

▼ **8** *In this study of a lake in Donegal, Ireland, by Adrian Smith, you can see the way the blurring of the paint captures the effect of hazy, rain-laden clouds.*

SUNNY DAYS

Working out of doors on a bright sunny day is a delightful experience. Brilliant sunlight casts emphatic shadows which can shift quite rapidly as the sun moves across the sky. The focus of your painting may suddenly be engulfed in shade, completely changing the composition. If you work quickly, you may complete the painting before the light changes. You will be forced to simplify the forms and tonal arrangements, to include only the essentials and edit out anything that is superfluous to the impact of the final image. Working directly from the subject in this concentrated way is an invaluable experience.

If time or your confidence doesn't permit you to complete a painting, you can make sketches and colour notes. These can be supplemented with reference photographs and all this material can be used in the studio later.

Bright light can be so dazzling that you can't see the subject clearly. And changing light on your working support can make it difficult to accurately assess tonal and colour relationships. Ideally, you should try to find a shaded spot – under a tree or a café awning, or in the shadow of a building, for example. Failing that, a large-brimmed hat or a parasol will protect your eyes from the glare and give you a neutral light to work in. The artist in a panama isn't posing; he or she is adopting a sensible working practice.

The strength and direction of sunlight affect the appearance of things. If the sun is in front of you, buildings and objects are thrown into shadow and colours will have a coolish cast. Light from behind the observer is generally warmer in colour and objects bathed in sunlight appear warmer and nearer. Side-lighting creates the most striking shadows and throws forms and textures into high relief. When the sun is overhead the opposite happens: shadows are reduced to a minimum, while forms and textures appear flatter. Dawn and sunset provide some wonderfully dramatic backlit effects.

You can see this in John Lidzey's picture on page 81. The demonstrations by Albany Wiseman, on pages 82 and 85, show how dramatically sunlight can change in a short time and what a difference this makes to the appearance of things.

▶ *'Harbour, Mount Deya' by David Curtis. The artist has captured the unique sun-drenched warmth of a Mediterranean village. He has used a palette of pale ochry yellows, which are contrasted with blues and blue-greens of sea and sky. The sun is high in the sky, casting intense but limited shadows such as those directly under the boat and under the awning of the taverna. Again, the brilliance of the white watercolour paper creates the luminosity of light and also unifies the entire image.*

▼ *The artist Bill Taylor has created a different kind of bright light. This time it is the cool bright light of winter. Cool blue shadows are contrasted with warmer areas of sunlight. Long crisp shadows thrown on to the rooftops and the ground tell you that the sun is low in the sky.*

▼ In 'Sunlight Façade' by Ian Sidaway, strong bright sunlight from the side casts intense dark shadows. These, together with the dark interiors seen through the window and doorway, provide an important compositional motif.

The crisp forms and the contrast between the light and dark areas heighten the sense of sun and light. The dark shadows and the spattered texturing on the façade allow us to read white paper as light on a white surface.

ARCHITECTURE AND LIGHT

I asked the artist Tig Sutton to find a subject that expressed an aspect of light. He chose this enchanting pig, which can be found on a buttress on the south side of Lincoln Cathedral. It was a brilliantly sunny day in August and the sun was quite high in the sky. Deep shadows threw the architectural details into sharp relief. On a more overcast day they would not be seen with the same clarity.

The jostle of faces and forms that break up the solidity of the architectural mass provides an engaging subject. The artist particularly liked the mellow rosy colours of the weathered stone and the fact that, in places, the stonework is crumbling and grimy with soot. He wanted to capture the character of the stonework in his painting.

He had to look directly upwards to see the details of the subject, creating a dizzying perspective, emphasized by the way the two main figures loom over the ledge.

The artist likes to work on a large scale, so that he can stand back from the picture and view it from a distance. The painting measures 54 × 36 cm (22 × 14 in). He started by making a series of pencil sketches, which familiarized him with the subject and allowed him to investigate different compositional possibilities.

◀ *He started by making sketches of the subject. He did a drawing of the subject face-on for his own benefit, so that he could better understand what he was seeing in steep perspective. A roof and a spire were visible in the distance, but he removed these in order to create a more dramatic image.*

▶ *If you look closely you can see that the artist has captured the particular quality of the crumbling stone. He used a series of warm neutral washes to depict the rosy weathered stone. It is the contrast between the light and dark areas and the sharp edges of the shadows that conveys the brightness of the light.*

The tall format emphasizes the verticality of the architecture and makes for a bold composition. The bright blue sky provides a cool balance to the warm neutrals of the stone. The composition is carefully conceived. The eye is led from the base of the painting to the figure at the top. From there the angle of the ledge directs our attention to the sculpted form of the pig. The way the bright blue sky throws it into silhouette also arrests our attention.

INDEX